CW00840980

JOEL EMBIID

Kerrily Sapet

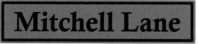

PUBLISHERS

2001 SW 31st Avenue
Hallandale, FL 33009

www.mitchelllane.com

First Edition, 2020.
Author: Kerrily Sapet
Designer: Ed Morgan
Editor: Lisa Petrillo

Series: Blue Banner Biographies
Title: Joel Embiid / by Kerrily Sapet

Hallandale, FL : Mitchell Lane Publishers, [2020]

Library bound ISBN: 9781680205039
eBook ISBN: 9781680205046

Contents

CHAPTER ONE

The Video

THE BASKETBALL COURT was tucked behind a row of apartments in Yaoundé, Cameroon. Cracks stretched like spiderwebs across its blacktop surface. The hoops at each end had broken rims. Most people in the West African country of Cameroon played soccer, not basketball. At 15 years old, Joel Embiid was no different—until a basketball coach spotted him. When Joel stepped onto the court and played for the first time, everything changed.

Standing at 6'9", Joel had grown tall like most basketball players, but he didn't know how to shoot or dribble. He bounced the ball off his foot, and had to chase it into the street. He let passes slip through his hands. Joel was terrible. But he loved the game, and wanted to learn more.

Joel's coach, Guy Moudio, gave him an old video of Hakeem Olajuwon, a legend in the National Basketball Association (NBA). The video showed basketball played like nothing Joel had seen before. To Joel, it looked like Olajuwon was dancing on the court. "I just fell in love with his game, his footwork, how he moves," said Joel. "I was so proud—I wanted to be like him, because he's African, moved from Nigeria to the U.S. I just felt if I had the chance, I would try to do the same thing."

Focus, hard work, and determination from a young age has helped Embiid be a success.

The video changed Joel's life. Joel told his coach that he wanted to be Olajuwon. For months, Joel watched the tape, rewinding it over and over as he studied Olajuwon's graceful, swift style of play. He tried to copy Olajuwon's moves—like the Dream Shake, where Olajuwon swayed his shoulders, slid past the guard, and scored.

To get stronger, Joel strapped on a weighted vest, stood near the bent rim of the basket, and jumped to catch balls his coach lobbed in the air time after time. Sometimes Joel cried from the pain. But he got better. Fast.

Joel Embiid's journey to the NBA was just beginning. Within a few years, he would be an NBA star, with people comparing him to Olajuwon. Playing on a glossy wooden court instead of a cracked blacktop court, Joel would set NBA records as thousands of fans chanted his nickname—"The Process."

Hakeem Olajuwon of the Houston Rockets takes on Shaquille O'Neal of the Orlando Magic at the NBA Finals in 1995.

Leap of Faith

ON MARCH 16, 1994, Joel Hans Embiid was born in Yaoundé, Cameroon. Joel's father, Thomas, was an officer in the Cameroon military. His mother, Christine, managed their home and cared for the family. Joel had a younger sister and brother, Muriel and Arthur. Like others in Yaoundé, the family spoke French, English, and Basaa, the native language of Cameroon.

Thomas and Christine taught their children to work hard. Joel washed his clothes by hand, even though the family had a maid. After school, he spent hours studying and memorizing his homework. Joel, nicknamed "JoJo," played volleyball in high school, dominating the court with his great height and athletic ability. He planned to play professional volleyball in France.

When basketball coach Guy Moudio suggested Joel play basketball, instead of volleyball, it took months to convince Joel's parents. Cameroon, a country of 23 million people, has only two indoor basketball courts. "Nobody plays basketball in Cameroon," his father Thomas said. Worried that basketball was a dead end, he wanted Joel to focus on school.

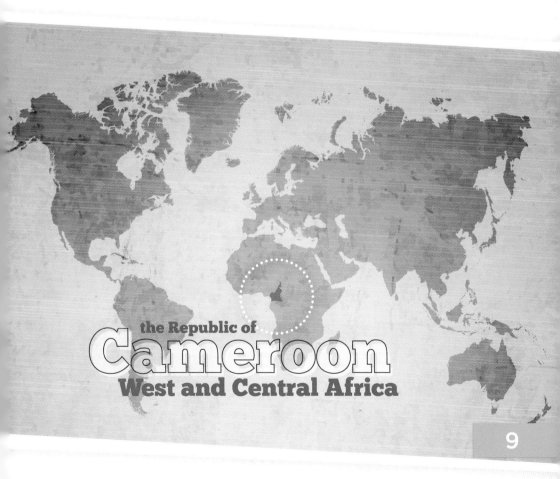

the Republic of
Cameroon
West and Central Africa

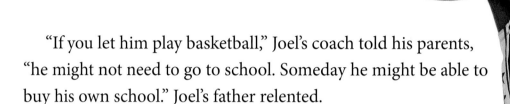

"If you let him play basketball," Joel's coach told his parents, "he might not need to go to school. Someday he might be able to buy his own school." Joel's father relented.

Skills Joel had learned from playing other sports helped him on the basketball court. Soccer and volleyball had taught him quick footwork, endurance, jumping, and blocking. Joel knew little about basketball, though. In the middle of his first game, he panicked, turned to Coach Moudio, and yelled, "What do I do? What do I do?"

Joel worked hard and learned quickly. Within weeks, he was hitting three-pointers and wrestling rebounds away from other players.

Coach Moudio suggested Joel attend a local basketball camp run by Luc Mbah a Moute, an NBA basketball player from Cameroon. Joel was too embarrassed to sign up, but Moudio registered him anyway. On the first morning of the camp, Joel was so nervous he stayed home. The next morning, his coach picked him up and took him there.

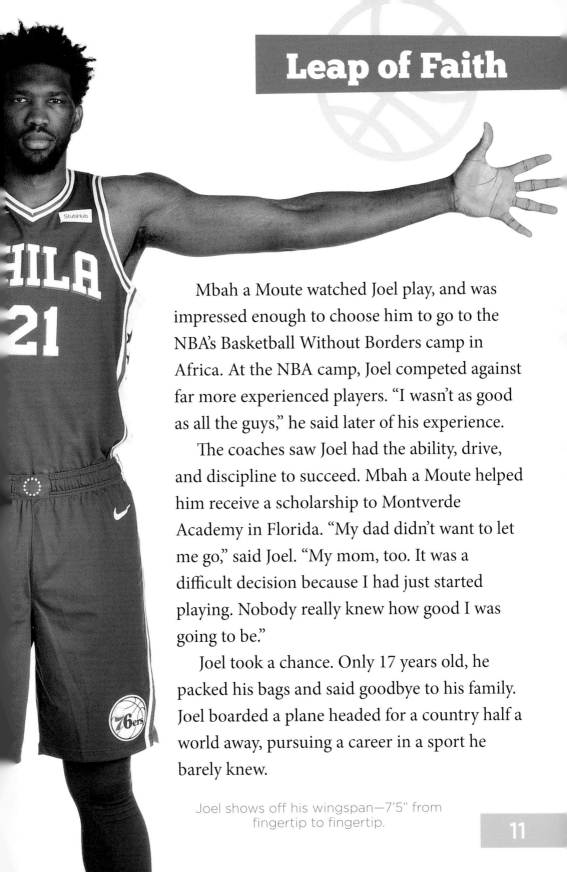

Leap of Faith

Mbah a Moute watched Joel play, and was impressed enough to choose him to go to the NBA's Basketball Without Borders camp in Africa. At the NBA camp, Joel competed against far more experienced players. "I wasn't as good as all the guys," he said later of his experience.

The coaches saw Joel had the ability, drive, and discipline to succeed. Mbah a Moute helped him receive a scholarship to Montverde Academy in Florida. "My dad didn't want to let me go," said Joel. "My mom, too. It was a difficult decision because I had just started playing. Nobody really knew how good I was going to be."

Joel took a chance. Only 17 years old, he packed his bags and said goodbye to his family. Joel boarded a plane headed for a country half a world away, pursuing a career in a sport he barely knew.

Joel shows off his wingspan—7'5" from fingertip to fingertip.

An Unknown from Cameroon

AT MONTVERDE ACADEMY, Joel faced challenges beyond just making new friends at a new school. He was living in a country where he didn't speak the language well, and didn't know anyone. But Montverde Academy was home to one of the best basketball programs in the United States. The team's head coach, Kevin Boyle, had developed NBA players.

Life on and off the basketball court was difficult for Joel. Lonely and homesick, he told his mom everything was fine, so she wouldn't worry. At practices, Joel's teammates laughed at him. He was clumsy and unpolished, compared to the other players who had played basketball for years. But Joel's coaches saw his raw talent.

One day, Coach Boyle gathered Joel's teammates and sent Joel to get a drink of water. "Laugh all you want," Boyle told them. "But in five years you're going to be asking him for a loan, because he's going to be worth about $50 million. You have no idea how good that kid is going to be."

During lunch breaks and after practices, Joel asked his coaches for extra help. He spent most of his free time in his room, studying videos of NBA stars. Joel was on the JV (junior varsity) team because of his lack of experience, and didn't get to play during games.

Joel needed to play more to get better. For his last year of high school, he transferred to The Rock School in Gainesville, Florida. Now 7' tall, he played the center position—shooting, passing, getting rebounds, and blocking passes. Joel led his team to the school's first state championship and was named the best high school center in his adopted country, the United States.

Embiid dunks past Javan Felix in a game against the Texas Longhorns in February 2014.

After graduating high school, Embiid began attending the University of Kansas in 2013, a basketball powerhouse. The university's coach, Bill Self, saw that Embiid could be brilliant on the court, even though he struggled to defend the hoop without fouling other players. "His basketball IQ is as high as anyone I've ever seen," said Self. "I've never been around anyone that's played less and known more. It's remarkable to watch."

During Embiid's first year at Kansas, he set a record for blocking 72 shots and averaging 11.2 points and 8.1 rebounds per game. He was named the Defensive Player of the Year. In March 2014, he suffered a small fracture in a bone in his back from the repeated strain of playing. He didn't need surgery, but he missed playing in the National Collegiate Athletic Association Tournament.

An Unknown from Cameroon

Although Joel had been playing basketball for just four years, scouts from NBA teams were watching him. "He can do things that only a few people in the world can do," said one of them. Joel felt ready to play at the next level, like the basketball idols he had watched over and over on video. On April 9, 2014, Embiid declared for the NBA draft.

Before the 2014 NBA draft, Embiid poses for a picture with hats from different teams at the NBA's headquarters in New York City.

Dark Days

AS **THE** **DAY** of the draft approached, people predicted Embiid would be the No. 1 overall pick—chosen first by the first team. But during a pre-draft work out with the Cleveland Cavaliers, he fractured a bone in his right foot. Just six days before the draft, he underwent surgery on his foot. Teams worried he was an injury prone "big man," the nickname for a center.

On June 26, 2014, the Philadelphia 76ers chose Embiid as the third draft pick. He was the third player in Cameroon's history to make it to the NBA. Although he wasn't well known in Cameroon, he had definitely become famous in the world of basketball.

Embiid signed his contract with the 76ers and began practicing with the team—shooting with his broken foot inside a protective boot. The 76ers knew Embiid would miss at least four months of the season due to his injury. He did rehabilitation exercises to strengthen his foot and watched his team from the sidelines.

On October 14, 2014, Embiid received tragic news. His 13-year-old brother, Arthur, had been killed when an out-of-control truck careened into a schoolyard. He hadn't seen Arthur since he left home at age 17. Embiid flew home, and mourned with his family.

After Arthur's funeral, Embiid returned to Philadelphia. He missed his brother and his family. Making matters worse, Embiid's foot was healing slowly. He had to sit out for the rest of the season, longing to play the sport he loved.

In 2015, tests showed that Embiid's foot wasn't healing properly. He underwent a second surgery. He would have to endure missing another season. Frustrated and angry, he did rehabilitation exercises but wasn't allowed to practice. He slept during the day and went out at night, hoping to avoid strangers asking about his injury. "I was a vampire," he said. Embiid watched as the 76ers lost 136 games.

Embiid thought about walking away from basketball. "All I wanted to do was go back home and never come back—just disappear and stay home," he said. But he knew his brother would not have wanted him to quit. From Cameroon to Philadelphia, people were waiting and hoping he would play again. The 76ers told Philadelphia fans to "Trust the Process," to be patient as the team rebuilt itself with young players.

As Embiid's foot healed, he realized he needed to "Trust the Process," too. "I think a lot about what I went through and how it prepared me to be a better man," he said. "I really feel like I'm The Process, like The Process is about me."

As the 2016–2017 season approached, doctors cleared Embiid to play. Fans, friends, and family would be watching as he finally stepped back onto the court. Two long, difficult years had come to an end.

Embiid stretches before the Philadelphia 76ers take on the Atlanta Hawks on January 7, 2016.

All-Star

ON **OCTOBER 26, 2016,** 852 days after he was drafted, Embiid played his first NBA game. His parents, home in Cameroon, stayed up late to watch the game. Philadelphia fans roared every time Embiid touched the ball. They chanted "Trust the Process" and gave him eight standing ovations. In just 22 minutes, Embiid scored 20 points and got 7 rebounds.

As 76ers fans cheer, Embiid reaches to score after beating players from the Houston Rockets to the net in January 2017.

Although the 76ers limited Embiid's playing time to rest his foot, he continued to get stronger. "He does things on a court that remind me of somebody that's able to hear music and just play the song," said Brett Brown, the 76ers head coach. "He will study another player, and all of a sudden it's a part of his game."

By January 2017, Embiid averaged 27 points, 10 rebounds, and 4 blocks per game—more than any other rookie. His numbers in those categories were higher than any rookie since 2011. One month later though, Embiid's left knee began to hurt. Tests showed a tear in his meniscus, the cartilage that cushions a knee. He had surgery, and was sidelined for the rest of the season, frustrated again by an injury.

When the 2017, 2018 season arrived, Embiid was ready. In November 2017, he set an NBA record. He scored 46 points and got 15 rebounds, 7 assists, and 7 blocks in one game in just 34 minutes. In the spring, he fractured a bone around his left eye, after colliding with a teammate, but was back on the court two weeks later. At the end of the season, Embiid was named to the NBA All-Star team.

When Embiid signed a five-year contract with the 76ers for $148 million—he knew he wanted to use the money to help others. He started a charity in Cameroon, called the Arthur Embiid and Angels Foundation, in his brother's memory. Today, Embiid's parents run the foundation that helps needy children, especially those from an orphanage in Yaoundé.

Embiid wears a protective face mask as he shoots over
Hassan Whiteside of the Miami Heat on April 19, 2018.

Embiid gives back because of the people who paved the way for him. He volunteers at Basketball Without Borders camps during the summers, hoping to inspire more children in Africa to play basketball. He also does charity work in Philadelphia.

"This is crazy, I still can't believe it," said Embiid. "It's just an example to show people anything is possible. That's my message I want to send to everybody. Anything is possible."

Joel Embiid once said his life is like a movie. It is the story of a teenager from Cameroon who overcomes difficulties and makes it to the NBA. But Joel Embiid's story isn't over. He is just getting started.

Embiid plays with children at the SOS Children's Village during the NBA's Basketball Without Borders Africa Camp in Ennerdale, South Africa.

Timeline

1994   Born in Yaoundé, Cameroon

2010   Begins playing basketball

2011   Goes to the Basketball Without Borders camp
           Begins attending Montverde Academy in Florida

2013   Attends the University of Kansas

2014   Undergoes surgery for a broken foot
           Drafted by the Philadelphia 76ers

2015   Has a second surgery on his foot

2016   Plays his first NBA game

2017   Has surgery on his knee
           Sets an NBA record for points, rebounds, assists, and blocks

2018   Makes his NBA playoffs debut
           Named a starter for the NBA All-Star Game

Quick Stats

Total Games Played	124
Total Games Won	73
Total Games Lost	51
Total Points Scored	2,878
Total Minutes Played	3,724
Average Points Per Game	23.2

Find Out More

Articles

Cohen, Ben. "How Joel Embiid Went from Volleyball Player to Basketball Sensation." *The Wall Street Journal*, November 16, 2017. https://www.wsj.com/articles/how-joel-embiid-went-from-volleyball-player-to-basketball-sensation-1510853198.

MacMullen, Jackie. "Cameroon Calling." *ESPN*, May 8, 2017. http://www.espn.com/espn/feature/story/_/page/presents19316766/the-key-joel-embiid-rise-luc-mbah-moute.

On the Internet

Joel Embiid Stats
http://www.espn.com/nba/player/_/id/3059318/joel-embiid

Joel Embiid Details, Articles, and Videos
http://www.nba.com/players/joel/embiid/203954

Joel Embiid and Basketball Without Borders
http://www.nba.com/article/2018/08/02/nba-africa-basketball-without-borders-camp-africa

https://www.nba.com/jazz/

Works Consulted

Aldridge, David. "A Process Toward Success: Joel Embiid Era Begins (At Last) in Philly." nba.com, November 21, 2016. http://www.nba.com/article/2016/11/21/morning-tip-joel-embiid-growth-player-philadelphia-76ers.

Basketball Without Borders Website
http://global.nba.com/basketball-without-borders/.

DeCourcy, Mike. "Joel Embiid's Pursuit of Hoops Greatness Not Just a Dream." *Sporting News*, January 22, 2014. http://www.sportingnews.com/us/ncaa-basketball/news/joel-embiids-pursuit-of-hoops-greatness-not-just-a-dream/wxyk1v6zv97t1pep47qnkyv1y.

Fondation Arthur Embiid & Angels Website.
http://arthurembiidandangels.org.

Jackson, Ryan. "Joel Embiid's Journey to One of the NBA's Most Dominant Big Men." foxsports.com, June 30, 2017. https://www.foxsports.com/nba/story/joel-embiid-s-journey-to-one-of-the-nba-s-most-dominant-big-men-010817?amp=true.

Jenkins, Lee. "Joel Embiid: 'I'm The Process.'" *Sports Illustrated*, October 26, 2016. https://www.si.com/nba/2016/10/26/joel-embiid-philadelphia-76ers-the-process.

King, Jason. "Meet Kansas' Joel Embiid, a Cameroon Native Blossoming into a Top NBA Prospect." *Bleacher Report*, December 17, 2014. https://bleacherreport.com/articles/1891203-meet-kansas-joel-embiid-a-cameroon-native-blossoming-into-a-top-nba-prospect.

MacMullan, Jackie. "Joel Embiid is More than the NBA's Best Follow." *ESPN*, October 31, 2017. http://www.espn.com/nba/story/_/id/21237211/nba-joel-embiid-more-nba-best-follow.

Powell, Shaun. "Hoops Journey of Philadelphia 76ers Phenom Joel Embiid a Storybook-like 'Process.'" nba.com, October 18, 2017. http://www.nba.com/article/2017/10/17/joel-embiid-goes-volleyball-star-budding-presence-philadelphia-76ers.

Rappaport, Max. "If Joel Embiid is The Process, His Debut Proved We Should Trust Him." complex.com, October 27, 2016. https://www.complex.com/sports/2016/10/joel-embiid-trust-the-process.

Index

About the Author

Kerrily Sapet is the author of more than 20 nonfiction books and numerous magazine articles for kids. Born in Indiana, a state nicknamed the "cradle of basketball," Sapet grew up playing basketball in the driveway with her father. She currently lives near Chicago, with her husband and two sons.